Liebe Schülerin, lieber Schüler!

Das Einprägen **unregelmäßiger Verben** und ihrer Vergangenheitsformen ist von großer Bedeutung für die Beherrschung der englischen Sprache.

Anhand spannender Abenteuer aus Robin Hood's Leben lernst und übst Du in diesem Lernprogramm etwa die Hälfte aller unregelmäßigen Verben. (Im Teil II lernst Du die restlichen kennen.)

Das Programm ist so aufgebaut, daß Du **allein** damit arbeiten kannst. Unter jeder Aufgabe befindet sich ein **graues Feld mit der Lösung.** Am Rand findest Du die Übersetzung wichtiger Wörter zum Textverständnis.

Wie ist das Programm aufgebaut?

Die Arbeit mit dem Übungsbuch sollte **auf 6 Tage verteilt** werden. Nach jedem Übungsabschnitt findest Du einen **Zwischentest**. Damit kannst Du prüfen, ob Du an diesem Tag erfolgreich gelernt hast. Die **Lösungen** dazu findest Du auf dem **letzten Blatt**, das Du jedoch erst anschauen darfst, wenn Du mit allen Aufgaben eines Zwischentests fertig bist.

Auf der **Rückseite** des Blattes, das Du jetzt gerade liest, findest Du den **Abschlußtest**. Bearbeite ihn, nachdem Du das ganze Programm durchgearbeitet hast, also am 7. Tag! Die **Lösungen** dazu findest Du ebenfalls **auf dem letzten Blatt** dieses Buches.

Und noch etwas: Du könntest natürlich leicht schwindeln, indem Du einfach die Antworten aus dem grauen Feld abschreibst – aber dann wäre der Lernerfolg bei weitem nicht so groß, als wenn Du Deine **eigenen Lösungen aufschreibst** und **dann erst mit der Antwort vergleichst**.

Was ist beim Gebrauch des Programms unbedingt zu beachten?

1. Die **Lösungen** stehen jeweils im **grauen Feld** unter den einzelnen Aufgaben. Man **deckt** sie am besten mit einem Blatt **ab.**
2. **Die Antworten** werden **ins Programm geschrieben.** Man kann sie aber auch auf ein **Blatt schreiben,** wenn das Programm öfters verwendet werden soll; z. B. von Geschwistern, zur späteren **Wiederholung** oder bei **klassenweisem Einsatz.**
3. Du mußt die **eigenen Antworten nach jedem Lernschritt genau** mit den Lösungen im grauen Feld **vergleichen.**
4. **Unbekannte Wörter** findest Du in der Regel **am Rand** auf grauem Grund. Notfalls kannst Du in einem englisch-deutschen Wörterbuch nachschlagen.
5. **Pro Tag** nicht mehr als **einen Übungsteil** bearbeiten!

Viel Freude und Erfolg bei der Arbeit!

ABSCHLUSSTEST

S e t z e die Verben im **Simple Past** e i n !

1. ⟨gehen⟩ Yesterday Samuel __________ to see his friend Charly.
2. ⟨füttern⟩ Last winter we _________ the birds every day.
3. ⟨nehmen⟩ The waitress __________ my £ 10 note but she didn't bring me any change.
4. ⟨verlassen⟩ Christopher Columbus _________ Europe on August 3rd, 1492.
5. ⟨verbringen⟩ Last summer we _________ our holidays in the Alps.

S e t z e das **Past Participle** e i n !

6. ⟨sehen⟩ The gangsters were __________ when they left the flat.
7. ⟨zerbrechen⟩ The vase was __________ by Keith.
8. ⟨verlieren⟩ The fight was __________ before it had started.
9. ⟨treffen⟩ I have not _________ my friend Brian for two years.
10. ⟨bekommen⟩ The workers have not _________ any money since Christmas.
11. ⟨sinken⟩ The ship has _________ .
12. ⟨sagen⟩ Tony has __________ that he likes hiking.

S e t z e die **richtigen Formen** e i n !

Grundform	**Simple Past**	**Past participle**	**deutsch**
throw	threw	thrown	werfen
win	__________ (13)	__________ (14)	__________ (15)
__________ (16)	__________ (17)	slept	__________ (18)
__________ (19)	__________ (20)	told	__________ (21)
__________ (22)	became	__________ (23)	__________ (24)

1. ROBIN'S CHILDHOOD

Robin Hood lived in this house as a boy

Robin and his parents lived in a house on the edge of Sher-	am Rande
wood Forest. Sherwood Forest was one of the largest of	
England's forests with lots of wild deer. Only the kings of	Rotwild, Hirsche
England had the right to hunt the deer. The King employed	jagen / beschäftigte
foresters who kept guard over these deer and Robin's father	Wacht
was the head forester of Sherwood Forest.	Oberförster
Robin spent a very happy childhood in the forest. His	Kindheit
father showed him how to shoot with a bow and arrow.	Pfeil und Bogen
This was an important part of his education because these	Erziehung
were lawless times. His mother taught him to be polite, to	gesetzlose Zeiten
be truthful and, as he grew older, to read and write. Robin's	ehrlich
childhood friends were the children of the other foresters,	
but his favourite companion was a girl called Marian whose	liebster Spielgefährte
father was the Earl of Huntingdon. Robin's father, however,	Graf / jedoch
made some enemies, and some of them told lies to the king	Feinde / Lügen
about him. They caused him to be arrested, and he was	veranlaßten
thrown into prison. A few months later he died. Robin and	Gefängnis / starb
his mother were now alone. One night there was a loud	
knock at the door. When they opened it, they were con-	klopfen / standen ge-
fronted by five men. All of them wore the livery of the	genüber / Uniform

King's foresters. The leader came into the room and said, "I'm the new head forester. This house is now mine and you two will have to leave."

Fortunately one of Robin's uncles lived only a few miles away and so they went to his house. Uncle Gamewell made them very welcome. Robin lived there for many years, but his mother died very soon after they had arrived.

leader	Führer
mine	das meine
Fortunately	glücklicherweise

S u c h e aus dem Text "Robin's Childhood" die fehlende Form und s e t z e sie in die Lücken e i n !

1

teach	taught	taught
lehren	lehrte	gelehrt

His mother taught him to be polite.

2

tell	____________	told
erzählen	erzählte	erzählt
sagen	sagte	gesagt

Some enemies ____________ lies about Robin Hood's father.

1

3

come	____________	come
kommen	kam	gekommen

The leader of the foresters ____________ into the room.

4

keep	____________	kept
(be-)halten	(be-)hielt	gehalten (behalten)

The foresters ____________ guard over the deer in Sherwood Forest.

---

2. told 3. came 4. kept

5
grow | ________ | grown
werden, wachsen | wurde, wuchs | geworden, gewachsen
When Robin ________ older he learnt to read and write.

6
show | ________ | shown
zeigen | zeigte | gezeigt
Robin's father ________ him how to shoot an arrow.

7
wear | ________ | worn
(Kleidung) tragen | trug | getragen
The men ________ the livery of the King's foresters.

2

8
say | ________ | said
sagen | sagte | gesagt
The leader ________, "I'm the new head forester."

5. grew   6. showed   7. wore   8. said

9
throw | threw | ________
werfen | warf | geworfen
Robin's father was ________ into prison.

10
spend | ________ | spent
verbringen | verbrachte | verbracht
Robin ________ a very happy childhood in the forest.

3

11
make | ________ | made
machen | machte | gemacht
Robin's father ________ some enemies.

12
go | ________ | gone
gehen, fahren | ging, fuhr | gegangen, gefahren
Robin and his mother ________ to his uncle who lived only a few miles away.

9. thrown   10. spent   11. made   12. went

S c h a u e n wir uns nun nochmal die ersten 12 Verben g e n a u e r a n ! Vielleicht hast Du schon bemerkt, daß bei einigen von ihnen die erste und zweite Vergangenheitsform gleich ist.

- E r g ä n z e die beiden Vergangenheitsformen!
- S c h r e i b e jeweils die Bedeutung des Verbs d a z u !

4

		Simple Past	Past Participle
1. say	(sagen)	said	said
2. tell	(______)	______	______
3. keep	(______)	______	______
4. make	(______)	______	______
5. teach	(______)	______	______
6. spend	(______)	______	______

2. (sagen, erzählen), told, told
3. (halten, behalten), kept, kept
4. (machen), made, made
5. (lehren), taught, taught
6. (verbringen), spent, spent

Bei folgenden drei Verben unterscheidet sich das Past Participle nur durch ein -n, das an die Grundform angehängt wird.
S e t z e die fehlenden Wörter e i n !

5

		Simple Past	Past Participle
1. grow	(wachsen)	grew	grown
2. ______	(______)	showed	______
3. ______	(______)	threw	______

2. show (zeigen) . . . , shown 3. throw (werfen) . . . , thrown

Sicher kannst Du nun auch die drei Zeitformen der noch verbleibenden drei Verben e i n s e t z e n . Du findest sie im Kreis.

		Simple Past	Past Participle
1. go	(gehen)	______	______
2. ______	(tragen)	______	______
3. ______	(kommen)	______	______

6

1. go, went, gone 2. wear, wore, worn 3. come, came, come

Übersicht

Setze nun die fehlenden Verbformen ein! (Bearbeite eine Zeile nach der anderen!)

7

Grundform	Simple Past	Past Participle
1. keep	___________	___________
2. ___________	told	___________
3. ___________	___________	shown
4. ___________	wore	___________
5. ___________	taught	___________
6. ___________	___________	thrown
7. spend	___________	___________
8. ___________	made	___________
9. grow	___________	___________
10. ___________	came	___________
11. ___________	___________	gone
12. ___________	___________	said

- Vergleiche zuerst **sorgfältig** mit den Lösungen!
- Decke dann mit der Hand (oder einem Blatt Papier) die zwei Vergangenheitsformen ab und sprich leise die 3 Formen!
- Arbeite erst weiter, wenn Du sie auswendig aufsagen kannst!

1. keep, kept, kept
2. tell, told, told
3. show, showed, shown
4. wear, wore, worn
5. teach, taught, taught
6. throw, threw, thrown
7. spend, spent, spent
8. make, made, made
9. grow, grew, grown
10. come, came, come
11. go, went, gone
12. say, said, said

S e t z e die Verben im Simple Past e i n !

When Robin was a boy he spent (1) most of his time in the forest. His father
verbrachte

__________ (2) a bow one day and __________ (3) him how to shoot with it.
machte zeigte

When he __________ (4) older his mother __________ (5) him to read and write.
wurde lehrte

But Robin's father had some enemies. They __________ (6) things about him that
erzählten

were not true. A few days later the sheriff __________ (7) with his men and
kam

__________ (8) Robin's father into prison.
warf

8

The next night there was a knock at the door. Five men __________ (9) into the
kamen

room and __________ (10), "You have to leave this house at once." They all
sagten

__________ (11) the livery of the King's foresters. So Robin and his mother
trugen

__________ (12) to Uncle Gamewell.
gingen

2. made	3. showed	4. grew	5. taught
6. told	7. came	8. threw	9. came
10. said	11. wore	12. went	

Und hier sind noch einige Übungen, die inhaltlich nichts mit der Robin Hood Story zu tun haben.
L i e s zuerst den Fragesatz und s e t z e dazu das fettgedruckte Verb in der richtigen Form im Antwortsatz e i n !

1 When **did** you **come** to Germany last year?
We came ______ at Easter.

2 When **did** he **show** you his photos?
He ______ me the photos last Saturday.

3 When **did** she **tell** you this story?
She ______ it to me last week.

4 When **did** you **wear** this dress for the last time?
I ______ it last month, when I ______ to the theatre.

5 What **did** she **say** about me?
She ______ only good things about you.

6 When **did** you **make** this cake?
I ______ it last Sunday.

7 **Did** you **spend** more money last holiday or this year?
I ______ a lot more money this year.

---

2. showed 3. told 4. wore, went 5. said 6. made 7. spent

Zwischentest A

L i e s die Fragen zuerst und s e t z e dann das Verb im Antwortsatz in der **richtigen Zeit** e i n !

1 Where did Robin spend his childhood?

He ___________ it in Sherwood Forest.

2 Did his father or his mother show him how to shoot with a bow and arrow?

His father ___________ him to shoot with a bow and arrow.

3 What did his mother teach him?

She ___________ him to be polite and to read and write.

4 To whom did the enemies tell lies about Robin's father?

They ___________ lies to the king.

5 What did the foresters in Sherwood forest wear?

They ___________ the King's livery.

6 Did all of the foresters come into the room or only their leader?

Only the leader ___________ into the house.

7 What did the leader say?

He ___________ , "This is my house now. You have to leave!"

8 Where did Robin and his mother go?

They ___________ to Uncle Gamewell.

W ä h l e die richtigen Verben a u s und s e t z e sie im **Simple Past** e i n !

grow – keep – make – throw

9. Liz ___________ fewer mistakes than Pete.

10. My grandfather ___________ thirty canaries in cages.

11. John ___________ the paper out of the window.

12. This tree ___________ two metres in 5 years.

Die **Lösungen** findest Du am **Ende** dieses Programms.

2. HOW ROBIN BECAME AN OUTLAW

Geächteter

As Robin grew up he learned how to defend himself. With his bow and arrow he could easily hit the centre of a target from about 220 ft. He could also ride as well as any of the King's foresters. He never forgot, however, how his father had lost his position and then his home. One day a friend told him about an archery contest to be held at the next Nottingham fair. Robin made up his mind to enter this contest and to go to Nottingham. He took with him his best bow and his straightest arrows and set out for the fair. As he was passing through the forest he met a group of foresters who asked him where he was going. They told him that nobody was allowed to carry a bow or arrows in the forest.

verteidigen
treffen / Zielscheibe
Stelle
Bogenschützenwettbewerb / Jahrmarkt
geradesten

Robin answered, "I'm going to the Nottingham archery contest to win the first prize, the silver arrow." The leader of the group laughed and said, "Can you see that herd of deer over there? If you can shoot only half as far as them, I will call you a good archer." Robin raised his bow and shot an arrow. The leader of the deer herd fell dead.

Preis
Bogenschütze
tot

"You've killed one of the King's deer," shouted one of the foresters, "and the penalty for that is death." They tried to catch Robin, but he was too quick for them. He ran as fast as he could, swung over a fallen tree and found some thick brambles which hid him from view. As the foresters didn't have any dogs with them they soon lost his trail and eventually gave up the chase. When they had gone Robin crept out again. But Robin knew now that he was outlawed and anyone could kill him for a reward if they wanted.

Naturally the King's foresters were the most eager to catch him.

penalty	Strafe
brambles	Brombeergestrüpp
trail	Fährte
eventually / chase	schließlich / Jagd
outlawed	geächtet
reward	Belohnung
the most eager	die eifrigsten

Setze die passenden Verbformen ein! Lies, wenn nötig, nochmal im Text nach!

1

shoot	________	shot
schießen	schoß	geschossen

Robin ________ an arrow at the leader of the deer.

2

lose	lost	________
verlieren	verlor	verloren

Robin's father had ________ his job.

3

fall	________	fallen
fallen	fiel	gefallen

The deer ________ because it was shot.

4

hold	held	________
halten	hielt	gehalten
stattfinden	fand statt	stattgefunden

An archery contest was ________ at the Nottingham fair.

1. shot 2. lost 3. fell 4. held

5

take	__________	taken
nehmen	nahm	genommen

Robin __________ his best bow and straightest arrows with him.

6

meet	__________	met
(an-)treffen	traf (an)	(an-) getroffen

Robin __________ a group of foresters on his way to Nottingham.

11 **7**

know	__________	known
wissen, können, kennen	wußte, konnte, kannte	gewußt, gekonnt, gekannt

Robin __________ now that he was an outlaw.

8

run	__________	run
rennen	rannte	gerannt
laufen	lief	gelaufen

Robin __________ as fast as he could.

5. took	6. met	7. knew	8. ran

9

swing	________	swung
(sich) schwingen	schwang (sich)	(sich) geschwungen

Robin ________ over a fallen tree.

10

become	________	become
werden	wurde	geworden

Robin ________ an outlaw.

11

hide	________	hidden
verstecken	versteckte	versteckt

Robin ________ behind some thick brambles.

12

find	________	found
finden	fand	gefunden

Robin ________ some thick brambles.

9. swung 10. became 11. hid 12. found

13

creep	________	crept
kriechen	kroch	gekrochen

When the foresters had gone Robin ________ out of the brambles.

14

give up	________ up	given up
aufgeben	gab auf	aufgegeben

After 30 minutes the foresters ________ up the chase.

15

forget	________	forgotten
vergessen	vergaß	vergessen

Robin never ________ how his father lost his position.

13. crept	14. gave	15. forgot

DAS BESONDERE VERB

Ein unregelmäßiges Verb dieses Kapitels fehlt uns noch. Vorne im Text kommt es viermal vor. Setze ein!

16

Robin Hood __________ easily hit the centre of a target.

He __________ ride as well as a King's forester.

He was outlawed and anyone __________ kill him.

14

He ran as fast as he __________ .

can	__________ [kud]
können	konnte

Es ist deshalb ein besonderes Verb, weil es nur die Simple Past-Form davon gibt, also kein Past Participle. Man muß also, wenn man z. B. einen Satz im Present Perfect bilden will, auf "to be able to" ausweichen.

Beispiel: Robin Hood **has been able to** hit the centre of the target.

16. could

Und nun findest Du die unregelmäßigen Verben dieses Kapitels geordnet. Zunächst s c h a u e n wir uns Verben a n , bei denen Simple Past und Past Participle gleich sind.

	Simple Past	Past Participle
1. creep (kriechen)	crept	crept
2. meet (treffen)	__________	__________
3. lose (verlieren)	__________	__________
4. find (finden)	__________	__________
5. hold (halten)	__________	__________
6. swing (schwingen)	__________	__________
7. shoot (schießen)	__________	__________

15

2. met, met 3. lost, lost 4. found, found
5. held, held 6. swung, swung 7. shot, shot

S e t z e auch bei folgenden drei Verben die fehlenden Formen e i n !

	Simple Past	Past Participle
1. give (geben)	gave	given
2. hide (verstecken)	hid	__________
3. fall (fallen)	fell	__________
4. take (nehmen)	took	__________
5. forget (vergessen)	forgot	__________

16

Frage: Kannst Du erkennen, was diese 5 Verben gemeinsam haben?

Antwort: Alle Past Participles ____________________(6).

2. hidden 3. fallen 4. taken 5. forgotten
6. . . . haben am Ende ein **-en**. (Oder: . . . enden mit einem **-en**)

17

Kannst Du die Buchstaben vom Baum richtig in die Wörter einsetzen?

	Present	Simple Past	Past Participle
1. (werden)	bec ◯ me	bec ◯ me	bec ◯ me
2. (wissen)	kn ◯ w	kn ◯ w	kn ◯ wn

1. bec(o)me bec(a)me bec(o)me
2. kn(o)w kn(e)w kn(o)wn

18

Setze die fehlenden Verben in der Simple Past-Form ein!

When Robin was 10 years old he __________ (konnte) (1) easily hit the centre of a target. He never __________ (vergaß) (2) how his father __________ (verlor) (3) his job as a forester. One day the king __________ (hielt ab) (4) an archery contest at Nottingham fair. Robin __________ (nahm) (5) his bow and set out for the fair. On his way he __________ (traf) (6) a group of foresters. One of them said to him, "If you can shoot half as far as that herd of deer, I will call you a good archer." Robin __________ (schoß) (7) and the leader of the deer herd __________ (fiel) (8) dead. Robin __________ (rannte) (9) away. He __________ (fand) (10) some thick brambles and __________ (versteckte sich) (11) behind them. The foresters soon __________ (verloren) (12) the trail and after a few hours search they __________ (gaben) (13) up. Robin __________ (kroch) (14) out again but he __________ (wußte) (15) that every man __________ (konnte) (16) kill him if he wanted.

1. could	2. forgot	3. lost	4. held	5. took	6. met
7. shot	8. fell	9. ran	10. found	11. hid	12. lost
13. gave	14. crept	15. knew	16. could		

Übersicht

Setze nun die fehlenden Verbformen ein! (Bearbeite eine Zeile nach der anderen!)

1.	________	fell	________
2.	________	________	held
3.	________	found	________
4.	swing	________	________
5.	________	________	met
6.	shoot	________	________
7.	________	could	✕
8.	lose	________	________
9.	________	knew	________
10.	________	took	________
11.	________	________	become
12.	hide	________	________
13.	________	crept	________
14.	forget	________	________

- Vergleiche zunächst sorgfältig mit den Lösungen!
- Decke dann mit der Hand (oder einem Blatt Papier) die zwei Vergangenheitsformen ab und sprich leise die 3 Formen!
- Arbeite erst weiter, wenn Du alle auswendig aufsagen kannst!

1. fall, fell, fallen
2. hold, held, held
3. find, found, found
4. swing, swung, swung
5. meet, met, met
6. shoot, shot, shot
7. can, could
8. lose, lost, lost
9. know, knew, known
10. take, took, taken
11. become, became, become
12. hide, hid, hidden
13. creep, crept, crept
14. forget, forgot, forgotten

Und nun noch einige Übungen mit unregelmäßigen Verben, die keinen Bezug zur Robin Hood Story haben.
S c h a u Dir die Bilder a n ! Was haben die Menschen bzw. Tiere soeben getan?
U n t e r s t r e i c h e die richtige Form und s e t z e diese dann in die Lücke e i n !

lose-lost-lost

1. This lady has ____________ her purse on the way to the supermarket.

hide-hid-hidden

2. The squirrel has ____________ the nuts under the bush.

find-found-found

3. Richard and Annette have ____________ a lot of Easter eggs.

1. lost 2. hidden 3. found
(Das Present Perfect bildet man also immer mit dem Past Participle.)

V e r v o l l s t ä n d i g e auch folgende Sätze im Present Perfect!

1. This bird ______ __________ out of its nest.

2. I haven't __________ this friend for 5 years.

3. Nobody ______ __________ this taxi yet.

1. has fallen   2. met   3. has taken

Zwischentest B

1 Who did Robin meet when he went through the forest?

He __________ the King's foresters.

2 What did he take with him to Nottingham?

He __________ with him his bow and straightest arrows.

3 How did Robin kill the deer?

He __________ an arrow.

4 Where did Robin hide from the foresters' view?

He __________ behind some thick brambles.

5 What did Robin do when the foresters had gone?

He __________ out again.

V e r v o l l s t ä n d i g e folgende Sätze im **Present Perfect**!

fall – swing – lose – find

6. This monkey ________ __________ from one tree to the next.

7. Jeff ________ __________ a pound note in the waste paper basket.

8. This child ________ __________ from its bike.

9. These two hikers ________ __________ their way.

S e t z e die Verben im **Simple Past** e i n !

can – know – give – run

10. The girl __________ not ride the horse.
11. Francis __________ faster than all his friends.
12. I think, his parents __________ him too much money when he was a boy.
13. Today Susan __________ everything the teacher asked her.

Die **Lösungen** findest Du am **Ende** dieses Programms.

3. THE ARCHERY CONTEST AT NOTTINGHAM

Bogenschützenwettkampf

Robin could not go to the contest now without some kind of disguise. He obtained some old clothes which he got from a country inn, called "The Blue Boar" and put these on. When Robin had finished disguising himself even his own mother would not have known him.

Verkleidung / beschaffte sich / Landgasthaus

The roads to Nottingham were crowded with people as the contest had raised much interest. As the competitors began to take their places, Robin took a look around and saw Marian, his boyhood sweetheart, sitting in the box next to the King. Now more than ever Robin wanted to win the silver arrow in order to present it to her.

voll von Leuten
Rivalen
Jugendliebe
um zu schenken

When the contest started the man next to Robin had a green bandage over his left eye and the clothes that he wore were even older than Robin's. Gradually, as the contest proceeded, each target was moved further away from the bowmen until finally only Robin and the stranger were in the competition. His rival shot first and his arrow struck the very centre of the target. Robin took careful aim and his arrow flew to the target and split the shaft of his rival's arrow.

Binde
allmählich / fortschritt
Bogenschützen
zielte sorgfältig
Schaft

So Robin won the contest and got the silver arrow which he then presented to Marian. "I thank you, dear friend," she said with a sweet smile. After the contest Robin left Nottingham as fast as he could. Once again he went to the "Blue Boar" in Sherwood Forest. Inside the inn were about twenty men who sang and drank noisily, their bows and arrows discarded against the walls. Robin sat down and ordered a meal. Suddenly he saw, among the crowd, the man with the green bandage. He also recognized Robin at the same moment. "This is the man, who beat the best archers in England today," he shouted. "He won the silver arrow and gave it to Maid Marian. Let's make him our leader." The others did not believe him at first. But when he swore on oath that this was true, all of them took up the cry, and shouted, "Robin Hood shall be our leader in the greenwood."

überreichte
„Blauer Eber"
lärmend
abgelegt
wiedererkannte
Anführer / glauben
Eid
Laubwald

Setze jeweils das Verb in der richtigen Form ein!
Lies dazu, wenn nötig, nochmal im Text nach!

1

sing	___________	sung
singen	sang	gesungen

About twenty men ___________ in the inn.

2

fly	___________	flown
fliegen	flog	geflogen

His arrow ___________ to the target.

3

sit	___________	sat
sich setzen	setzte sich	sich gesetzt

Robin ___________ down and ordered a meal.

---

1. sang 2. flew 3. sat

4

get	____________	got
bekommen	bekam	bekommen

Robin ____________ some old clothes from a country inn.

5

beat	____________	beaten
besiegen	besiegte	besiegt

Robin ____________ the best archers of England.

23

6

strike	____________	struck
(ein-)schlagen	schlug (ein)	(ein-)geschlagen
treffen	traf	getroffen

The man's arrow ____________ the very centre of the target.

7

drink	____________	drunk
trinken	trank	getrunken

The men sat in the inn and ____________ wine and beer.

4. got 5. beat 6. struck 7. drank

8

put on	____________	put on
anziehen (Kleidung)	zog an	angezogen

Robin ____________ old clothes in the inn.

9

swear	____________	sworn
schwören	schwor	geschworen
fluchen	fluchte	geflucht

The man ____________ that Robin was the winner of the silver arrow.

24

10

split	____________	split
spalten	spaltete	gespalten

Robin's arrow ____________ the shaft of his rival's arrow.

8. put on 9. swore 10. split

11

see	____________	seen
sehen	sah	gesehen

Robin ____________ his boyhood sweetheart sitting in the box near the King.

12

begin	____________	begun
beginnen	begann	begonnen

The competitors ____________ to take their places.

13

win	____________	won
gewinnen	gewann	gewonnen

Robin ____________ the silver arrow and gave it to Maid Marian.

14

leave	____________	left
verlassen	verließ	verlassen
hinterlassen	hinterließ	hinterlassen

Robin ____________ Nottingham as fast as he could.

11. saw 12. began 13. won 14. left

Wir s e h e n uns nun diese 14 Verben nochmal g e n a u e r a n .
E r g ä n z e die fehlenden Formen! S c h r e i b e in die Klammern die d e u t s c h e B e d e u t u n g !

Grundform	Simple Past	Past Participle
1. win (gewinnen)	won	won
2. ______ (______)	struck	struck
3. ______ (______)	got	got
4. ______ (______)	sat	sat
5. ______ (______)	left	left

26

2. strike (schlagen, treffen) 3. get (bekommen)
4. sit (sitzen) 5. leave (verlassen, hinterlassen)

Bei folgenden 2 Verben sind **alle 3 Formen gleich.**
S c h r e i b e sie a u f !

1. ______ (anziehen) ______ ______
2. ______ (spalten) ______ ______

27

1. put on, put on, put on 2. split, split, split

S e t z e bei folgenden Verben das Past Participle e i n !
S c h r e i b e in die Klammern die d e u t s c h e B e d e u t u n g !

Grundform	Simple Past	Past Participle
1. beat (______)	beat	______
2. swear (______)	swore	______
3. see (______)	saw	______
4. fly (______)	flew	______

28

Frage: Welche Gemeinsamkeit haben die Past Participle-Formen?

Antwort: Ihr letzter Buchstabe ist ______ .

1. (schlagen) beaten 2. (schwören) sworn
3. (sehen) seen 4. (fliegen) flown
Antwort: Ihr letzter Buchstabe ist **ein -n.**

F ü l l e die fehlenden Buchstaben i n d i e L ü c k e n !
S c h r e i b e die d e u t s c h e B e d e u t u n g der Verben in die Klammern!

29 1. dr__nk (________________) dr__nk dr__nk
2. beg__n (________________) beg__n beg__n
3. s__ng (________________) s__ng s__ng

1. (trinken) i – a – u 2. (beginnen) i – a – u 3. (singen) i – a – u

Hast Du nun Lust auf ein kleines Kreuzworträtsel?
Das Lösungswort ergibt eine Stadt in England.
Du mußt hier auch Verben aus den vorhergehenden Kapiteln verwenden.

1. schlagen (Past Participle)
2. beginnen (Grundform)
3. kriechen (Simple Past)
30 4. treffen, begegnen (Simple Past)
5. sagen (Past Participle)
6. zeigen (Past Participle)
7. geben (Simple Past)
8. schießen (Simple Past)
9. fallen (Past Participle)
10. werden (Simple Past)

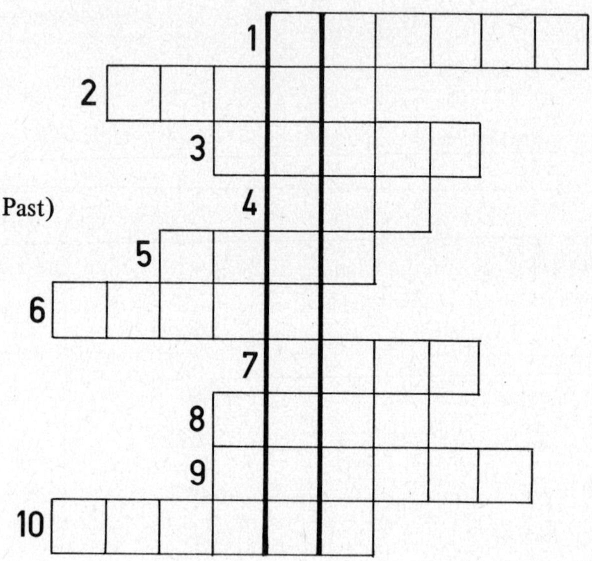

1. beaten	2. begin	3. crept	4. met	5. said
6. shown	7. gave	8. shot	9. fallen	10. became

Das Lösungswort ist: **Birmingham.**

Wie viele Fehler hast Du?

0 Fehler? Hervorragend
1–2 Fehler? Sehr gut
3 Fehler? Recht ordentlich

Wenn Du 4 und mehr Fehler hast, solltest Du nochmal das Kapitel 3 sorgfältig durcharbeiten.

Übersicht

S e t z e die fehlenden Verbformen e i n !

1. ________	struck	________		8. ________	flew	________
2. ________	got	________		9. beat	________	________
3. sit	________	________		10. ________	drank	________
4. ________	________	won		11. ________	________	sworn
5. sing	________	________		12. ________	________	begun
6. ________	________	seen		13. ________	put on	________
7. ________	________	left		14. ________	________	split

- V e r g l e i c h e nun sorgfältig mit den Lösungen!
- D e c k e dann mit der Hand (oder einem Blatt Papier) die zwei Vergangenheitsformen a b und s p r i c h l e i s e die 3 Formen eines Verbs!
- Arbeite erst weiter, wenn Du sie a u s w e n d i g aufsagen kannst!

1. strike	struck	struck	8. fly	flew	flown
2. get	got	got	9. beat	beat	beaten
3. sit	sat	sat	10. drink	drank	drunk
4. win	won	won	11. swear	swore	sworn
5. sing	sang	sung	12. begin	began	begun
6. see	saw	seen	13. put on	put on	put on
7. leave	left	left	14. split	split	split

S e t z e die fehlenden Verben im Simple Past e i n !

Robin __________ (1) some old clothes from a country inn and __________
bekam zog

them __________ (2). Then he __________ (3) to Nottingham. As the competitors
an ging

__________ (4) to take their places Robin looked around and __________ (5)
begannen sah

Maid Marian. The stranger's arrow __________ (6) the very centre of the target, but
traf

Robin's arrow __________ (7) right to the middle of the target too and __________
flog spaltete

(8) the shaft of his rival's arrow. So Robin __________ (9) the silver arrow which he
gewann

32 __________ (10) to Marian. After the contest Robin __________ (11) away from
gab rannte

Nottingham as fast as he __________ (12) and soon __________ (13) back to
konnte kam

the country inn. There he __________ (14) about twenty men who __________
traf sangen

(15) and __________ (16) noisily. Robin __________ (17) down and ordered a
tranken setzte sich

meal. Suddenly a man jumped up and shouted, "This is the man who __________
besiegte (schlug)

(18) the best archers of England." Then Robin recognized his rival.

1. got	2. put (them) on	3. went	4. began	5. saw
6. struck	7. flew	8. split	9. won	10. gave
11. ran	12. could	13. came	14. met	15. sang
16. drank	17. sat	18. beat		

Zwei besondere Verben sind to **get** und to **put**.
Schauen wir uns zunächst ihre Grundbedeutungen an:

to **get**	①	bekommen	②	verstehen
to **put**	③	setzen, legen, stellen		

Und hier ist zu jeder Bedeutung ein Beispielsatz:

33

○ I didn't **get** what she said.
○ **Put** the kettle on the stove, please.
○ Did you **get** your money from him?
○ Why didn't you **put** your wrist-watch in the cupboard?

Versuche, aus dem Sinnzusammenhang die richtige Bedeutung herauszufinden! Schreibe in den Kreis vor den Sätzen die richtige Nummer!

---

② Ich **verstand** nicht, was sie sagte.
③ **Stelle (Setze)** den Kessel auf den Ofen!
① **Bekamst** du dein Geld von ihm?
③ Warum hast du deine Armbanduhr nicht in den Schrank **gelegt**?

Diese beiden Verben haben in Verbindung mit verschiedenen Präpositionen (Verhältniswörtern) noch vielfältige Bedeutungen. Einige dieser Zusammensetzungen von **get** sehen wir uns gleich einmal an:

34

to get up	–	(vom Liegen) aufstehen
to get along with someone	–	sich mit jemand vertragen
to get on	–	einsteigen
to get off	–	aussteigen

- Arbeite erst weiter, wenn Du diese vier Bedeutungen beherrschst!
- Decke hierzu die linke Spalte (englische Wörter) zu und übersetze die deutschen Wörter in der rechten Spalte!

Und nun lernst Du einige wichtige Zusammensetzungen mit put kennen.
Lerne auch diese, bis Du sie gut beherrschst!

35

to put on	– anziehen (Kleidung)
to put somebody off	– jemand von etwas abbringen
to put forward	– vorschlagen
to put up	– aufbauen, aufstellen

Arbeite erst weiter, wenn Du durcheinander die deutschen Wörter übersetzen kannst!

36

Schau Dir nun die Bilder genau an! Setze dann die richtigen Zusammensetzungen mit to **put** ein!

1. This crane was ______ ____________ in one day.

2. Rod ______ ____________ the idea to go to a pub to drink a glass of beer.

3. Bill wanted to go to a cinema but he was ______ ____________ by his friend.

4. It was very cold outside. So Susie ______ ____________ her scarf, her boots and her warmest coat before she left the house.

1. put up	2. put forward	3. put off	4. put on

Ronald hatte in der vergangenen Woche einen Klassenausflug.
S e t ze die fehlenden Wörter e i n !

Last Friday Ronald had an outing with his class.	Ausflug
1. He ____________ (stand auf) at half past six.	
2. The class ____________ (traf sich) in the schoolyard at half past eight.	Schulhof
3. They ____________ (stiegen ein) the coach at a quarter to nine and they left at nine o'clock.	Bus
4. On the way the coach stopped only once. Most of the boys and girls ____________ (stiegen aus) and had an ice-cream.	einmal
5. When Ronald came home in the evening he was tired and happy. He had ____________ (vertrug sich) very well with his classmates.	müde Klassenkameraden

1. got up	2. met	3. got on	4. got off	5. got along

Und hier siehst Du Bilder aus Ronalds Fotoalbum.
S c h r ei b e zu jedem Foto einen p a s s e n d e n S a t z in der Vergangenheit!
(Simple Past)

1. The boys and girls ______ at a quarter to nine.

38

2. Most of ______

1. . . . **got on the coach** at a quarter to nine.
2. Most of **the children got off the coach to buy an ice-cream.**
(Auch ähnliche Sätze können richtig sein.)

In der folgenden Übung mußt Du einige Verben dieses und der vorigen Kapitel im Simple Past anwenden. Du erfährst dabei mehr über Ronalds Klassenausflug.

When the children __________ (1) the coach they pushed einstiegen	Bus / stießen
each other. On the coach they __________ (2) songs. The sangen	sich
teacher __________ (3) them to throw all the rubbish sagte, befahl	Abfall
into a bucket. Ronald __________ (4) beside his friend saß	Eimer / neben
Daisy on the coach. In Margate they __________ (5) a machten	
sandcastle on the beach. Their teacher __________ (6) zeigte	Sandburg
them the rare birds that __________ (7) over the sea. flogen	seltene
Daisy even __________ (8) a seal. When they had a sah	sogar / Seehund
break Ronald __________ (9) a tin of Coke and trank	Rast / Dose
__________ (10) a sandwich from Daisy. Then they bekam	
played cricket – and the boys __________ (11) the girls. besiegten, schlugen	
A few minutes before they __________ (12) back to kamen	
the coach it __________ (13) to rain. Everybody begann	
__________ (14) their anoraks. The coach arrived at the zogen an	
school late in the evening. When the boys and girls	spät
__________ (15) they __________ (16) quite a mess. ausstiegen hinterließen	ziemlich viel Schmutz
One girl nearly __________ (17) her sunglasses on the vergaß	fast / Sonnenbrille
coach. The coach driver __________ (18) because he had to fluchte	
pick up all the chewing-gum and paper from the floor of the coach.	Kaugummi

1. got on	2. sang	3. told	4. sat	5. made	6. showed
7. flew	8. saw	9. drank	10. got	11. beat	12. came
13. began	14. put on	15. left (got off)		16. left	17. forgot
18. swore					

Wie viele Wörter hast Du ganz **richtig**?

18–17: ausgezeichnet!
16–15: sehr gut!
14–13: recht gut!
12–11: Hast Du auch immer sorgfältig gearbeitet?
10 oder weniger: Studiere nochmal ab Lernschritt 22!

Zwischentest C

1 Where did Robin get his clothes for the disguise?

He ________ them in the "Blue Boar".

2 Who did he see sitting near the King?

He ________ Marian in the box near the King.

3 Where did the arrow of Robin's rival strike the target?

It ____________ the target right in the centre.

4 Did Robin or the man with the bandage win the contest?

Robin ________ it.

5 At first the men in the country inn didn't believe that Robin was the winner of the contest. Why did they finally believe?

Because he ________ on oath that it was true.

Was haben diese Leute **soeben** getan?
W ä h l e von den Verben im Rahmen a u s und s e t z e die richtige Form e i n !

split – drink – leave – sing – fly

6. This choir ________ ________ a nice song.

7. Roger ________ ________all this wood in three hours.

8. The astronauts ________ ________ the base.

9. I ________ ________ as many glasses of red wine as you.

10. This jet ________ ________ from London to New York in exactly 4 hours and 25 minutes.

S e t z e die richtigen Verben im **Simple Past** e i n !

begin - sit - put on - beat

11. Last weekend Nottingham Forest __________ Glasgow Rangers 3:0.
12. They __________ to laugh when they saw the clown.
13. Philipp __________ his coat and left the house.
14. The children __________ around the little dog and watched it.

Die **Lösungen** findest Du am **Ende** dieses Programms.

4. HOW ROBIN HOOD MET LITTLE JOHN

So Robin became the leader of the outlaws in the greenwood. His men swore to follow him whenever they heard the sound of his horn.

One day Robin had to cross a river which had been swollen by rains. A tree lay across it to act as a foot-bridge. Right in the middle of the tree Robin met a man who was much taller than Robin himself. Neither of them would allow the other to pass, and Robin became angry with the stranger. "Give way, fellow," he shouted. "No, I only give way to a man stronger than myself," replied the man. So a wild fight began. They fought with their cudgels and gave each other many hard blows. Finally, the stranger struck Robin on the head, and as his legs gave way he slipped and fell into the water. The giant looked down calmly as Robin sank under the water, but as soon as he came up to the surface again the man held out his cudgel to help him. Robin got hold of it and climbed back onto the bridge.
"You can hit hard," said Robin.
"So can you," answered the other man.

Geächtete
wann immer
dienen / genau
in der Mitte
keiner
Kerl
erwiderte
Keulen
Schläge
rutschte aus
Riese / ruhig
Oberfläche
zuschlagen

Robin blew his horn and his friends came out of the woods, each of them carrying his bow and arrow ready to shoot. Robin went up to the giant held out his hand and said, "Stranger, I'm Robin Hood. What's your name?"	Wälder bereit
The man began to laugh. He answered, "So you are Robin Hood? Well, my name is John Little. I've heard of your deeds and I've come to join you." "We need strong and noble fighters such as you," replied Robin. "From now on you will be known as Little John." Robin's men laughed loudly at this good joke.	Taten / sich anschließen edle Kämpfer Witz

---

Suche aus dem Text die fehlenden Formen und setze sie ein!
Lies, wenn nötig, im Text nochmal nach!

1

hear	___________	heard
hören	hörte	gehört

Robin's men came out of the greenwood whenever they ___________ the sound of his horn.

2

blow	___________	blown
blasen	blies	geblasen

When Robin ___________ his horn his friends came up to join him.

3

fight	___________	fought
kämpfen	kämpfte	gekämpft

Robin and Little John ___________ with their cudgels.

---

1. heard 2. blew 3. fought

4

sink	____________	sunk
sinken, untergehen	sank, ging unter	gesunken, untergegangen

Robin fell into the river and ____________ under the water.

41 **5**

lie	____________	lain
liegen	lag	gelegen

A tree ____________ across the river.

6

swell	swelled	____________
anschwellen	schwoll an	angeschwollen

The river had been ____________ by rains.

---

4. sank 5. lay 6. swollen

Im Kreis findest Du die Grundformen von bereits bekannten Verben, deren Simple Past und Past Participle sich mit den in diesem Kapitel gelernten Verben **reimen.** F ü l l e a l l e L ü c k e n a u s und schreibe in die Klammern die deutsche Bedeutung der Wörter im Kreis!

42

blow	blew	blown
1. ‹wachsen›	grew	grown
2. ‹____________›	____________	____________
3. ‹____________›	____________	____________

4. fight	____________	____________
5. ‹____________›	____________	____________

6. sink	____________	____________
7. ‹____________›	____________	____________

think
~~grow~~
drink
throw
fly

2. (oder 3.) ⟨werfen⟩ threw, thrown
3. (oder 2.) ⟨fliegen⟩ flew, flown
4. fought, fought
5. ⟨denken⟩ thought, thought
6. sank, sunk
7. ⟨trinken⟩ drank, drunk

Sicher hast Du schon gemerkt, daß in diesem Kapitel viele Verben vorkommen, die Du bereits kennengelernt hast. Zur Wiederholung üben wir diese Wörter nochmal.

S e t z e in die Erzählung neben die Bilder die Wörter in der richtigen Form e i n !

One day Robin Hood came (1) to a river.
A tree ______ (2) across it.

The river had been __________ (3) in the last few days.
Robin ______ (4) a tall man standing at the other side of the bridge.

They ______ (5) in the middle of the bridge.

As neither of them ______________ (6) a

wild fight _________ (7).

The stranger ___________ (8) Robin on his head.

Robin ________(9) into the water.

2. lay 3. swollen 4. saw 5. met 6. gave way 7. began
8. struck 9. fell

When Robin ____________ (1) the stranger ____________ (2) his cudgel to help Robin.
Robin ____________ (3) of it and climbed back on the bridge.

44

Robin ____________ (4) to the man, ____________ (5) his hand and ________ (6), "You can hit hard. What's your name?"
The stranger answered, "You're Robin Hood? I've ____________ (7) of your deeds and I've ________ (8) to join you."

1. came up	2. held out	3. got hold	4. went up
5. held out	6. said	7. heard	8. come

Übersicht

Setze die fehlenden Formen ein!

Grundform	Simple Past	Past Participle
1. ______	blew	______
2. ______	swelled	______
3. sink	______	______
4. hear	______	______
5. ______	______	lain
6. ______	______	fought

45

- Vergleiche zunächst sorgfältig mit den Lösungen!
- Decke dann mit der Hand (oder einem Blatt Papier) die zwei Vergangenheitsformen ab und lerne die 3 Formen auswendig!
- Arbeite erst weiter, wenn Du sie auswendig aufsagen kannst!

---

1. blow, blew, blown 2. swell, swelled, swollen 3. sink, sank, sunk
4. hear, heard, heard 5. lie, lay, lain 6. fight, fought, fought

---

Das besondere Verb

Von folgenden zwei Verben haben wir eines mit seinen Vergangenheitsformen kennengelernt. Kreuze es an!

46

☐	lie liegen	lay lag	lain gelegen
☐	lay legen	laid legte	laid gelegt

☒	lie	lay	lain

47

Man verwechselt diese beiden Verben leicht. Mit Hilfe einer Eselsbrücke kann man sich jedoch leicht merken, daß **liegen** auf englisch **lie** heißt. Schau Dir die ersten drei Buchstaben des deutschen Wortes an!
S c h r e i b e Deine Erkenntnis in einem Satz a u f !

Antwort: ______________________________

____

liegen beginnt mit denselben 3 Buchstaben wie **lie**.
deutsch: **lie**gen
englisch: **lie**

48

Last Sunday Albert and Alice went sailing. They had a bad accident. Here is their adventure in pictures.

Und hier siehst Du Albert und Alice, wie sie am nächsten Tag bei der Polizei über den Verlust ihres Segelbootes, das sie geliehen hatten, berichten. Fülle die Lücken aus! (Die Wörter in den Bildern helfen Dir.)

Yesterday we got a sailing boat from Shanks. First it was	Segelboot
very hot and we ______ (1)	
in the sun. We ______ (2) the yellow warning lights but we didn't know their meaning.	Warnlicht Bedeutung
Then we ______ (3)	
the thunder and the wind ______ (4) stronger and	Donner
stronger. The waves ______ (5) higher and higher. Suddenly a very high wave came over our boat and it	Wellen
______ (6). Fortunately we weren't too far away from the coast and we both were good swimmers. We	glücklicherweise
______ (7) against the waves and luckily reached the coast.	erreichten glücklich

1. lay 2. saw 3. heard 4. blew (grew) 5. grew 6. sank 7. fought

Zwischentest D

1 What did Robin and Little John do when they met on the tree?

They ________ with their cudgels.

2 What happened to Robin on the foot-bridge?

He slipped and ________ into the water.

3 What did Robin do to make his friends come out of the woods?

He ________ his horn.

4 Did his friends hear the horn or didn't they?

They ________ it at once.

S e t z e die fehlenden Verben im Simple Past e i n ! Wähle die richtigen aus!

take – sink – leave – lie – hear – swell – drink – fight

5. I played tennis and fell. Now my ankle is ________ .
6. The cat ______ in my bed all night.
7. The ship ________ just after the last passenger had left it.
8. Mr Redman ________ his wife's car and drove home.

Die **Lösungen** findest Du am **Ende** dieses Programms.

5. THE BUTCHER OF SHERWOOD FOREST

Metzger

Early one morning, while his friends were still asleep, Robin walked alone through Sherwood Forest. In the distance he saw a young man who was driving to Nottingham. He was seated on a cart which was drawn by a brown horse. When the man saw Robin he drew into the side of the road and stopped. He bent down from his cart and asked, “Are you going to the market? If so perhaps you would like to join me?”
“What have you got in your cart?“ asked Robin. “It’s full of meat,” answered the man. “I’m a butcher, you see.”
“Will you sell all of it?” Robin asked.
“You mean all the meat?” replied the butcher.
“No, I mean everything: the meat, the horse, the cart, and even your clothes,” said Robin. The butcher was very surprised, but as Robin offered to pay a good price he finally agreed to sell Robin everything and Robin was left with the meat, the sausages, the butcher’s clothes and last but not least, the horse and cart.

Once in Nottingham, Robin fed the horse, which then lay down and slept while Robin put up his stand near an entrance to the market. On the stand Robin hung up the sausages and built a pile of fresh meat from the pieces he had cut from the carcases. Then he advertised his wares

Ferne
Karren
begleiten
Metzger
Fleisch
überrascht / bot an
Würste
Eingang
Haufen (Stapel)
Fleischstücke / pries an

by calling to the passing crowd. “Fresh and tender meat, the best sausages in the country,” he cried. However Robin did not charge the same amount to everyone. He sold the meat to rich customers at £ 1.00 per piece, but allowed poor people to buy similar pieces for only 1 p or even gave it to them for nothing. Naturally, only poor people bought Robin’s meat and sausages.

Of course when other butchers at the market found out about Robin’s prices they nearly burst with anger. They got together and came to his stand where the biggest of them shouted, “Go back where you came from. You must have stolen all these goods.” Some of them broke his table and threw the meat and sausages to the ground. The biggest of them shook him and tore his clothes. Robin was unable to prevent these attacks because he was on his own. He sprang into his cart which was standing close by calling out as he drove away, “That’s how Robin Hood serves the people, he robs the rich to help the poor.” Then he drove along the streets and fled once more back into the greenwood.

For many years the people of Nottingham remembered his exploits and often retold the story.

zart
verlangen / Preis
Kunden
ähnliche / sogar
vor Wut platzen
Boden
verhindern / Angriffe / allein
behandeln
berauben
Taten

Setze jeweils das Verb in der richtigen Form ein! Lies dazu, wenn notwendig, nochmal im Text nach!

1

bend	___________	bent
sich beugen	beugte sich	sich gebeugt

The butcher ___________ down from his cart and asked, “Are you going to the market?”

2

hang	___________	hung
hängen	hängte	gehängt

Robin ___________ up the sausages.

3

buy	___________	bought
kaufen	kaufte	gekauft

Only poor people ___________ Robin’s meat and sausages.

1. bent | 2. hung | 3. bought

4

draw	drew	__________
ziehen, zeichnen	zog, zeichnete	gezogen, gezeichnet

The cart was __________ by a brown horse.

5

feed	__________	fed
füttern	fütterte	gefüttert 50

Robin __________ his horse with hay.

6

spring	__________	sprung
springen	sprang	gesprungen

Robin __________ into his cart.

4. drawn | 5. fed | 6. sprang

7

sell	__________	sold
verkaufen	verkaufte	verkauft

Robin __________ his meat in the market.

8

burst	__________	burst
(zer-)bersten	(zer-)barst	(zer-)borsten 51

The other butchers nearly __________ with anger.

9

steal	stole	__________
stehlen	stahl	gestohlen

Robin had not __________ the meat and the sausages.

7. sold | 8. burst | 9. stolen

52

10

break	___________	broken
(zer-)brechen	(zer-)brach	(zer-)brochen

Some of the butchers ___________ Robin's table.

11

sleep	___________	slept
schlafen	schlief	geschlafen

Robin's horse ___________ in the market.

12

cut	cut	___________
schneiden	schnitt	geschnitten

Robin had ___________ the meat in pieces.

10. broke 11. slept 12. cut

53

13

shake	___________	shaken
schütteln	schüttelte	geschüttelt

The biggest of the butchers ___________ Robin.

14

build	___________	built
bauen	baute	gebaut

Robin ___________ a pile of fresh meat.

15

tear	___________	torn
zerreißen	zerriß	zerrissen

The biggest butcher ___________ Robin's clothes.

16

flee	___________	fled
fliehen	floh	geflohen

Robin jumped in his cart and ___________ back into the greenwood.

13. shook 14. built 15. tore 16. fled

Folgende Verben haben eine Gemeinsamkeit. S c h r ei b e ihre drei Formen zunächst a u f !

	Grundform	Simple Past	Past Participle
1. brechen	break	______	______
2. fahren, treiben	______	______	______
3. stehlen	______	______	______
4. schütteln	______	______	______

54

Frage: Was haben diese 4 Verben gemeinsam?
Antwort: ____________________

1. break – broke – broken
2. drive – drove – driven
3. steal – stole – stolen
4. shake – shook – shaken

Ihre Past Participles enden mit **-en**.

In diesem Text lerntest Du zwei Verben kennen, bei denen alle drei Formen gleich sind.

Sie lauten: 1. c . . (schneiden) c____ c____

2. b . . . . (bersten) b______ b______

Auch in den vorigen Kapiteln lernten wir Verben kennen, bei denen alle drei Formen gleich sind. E r i n n e r s t Du Dich?

3. p____ ____ (anziehen)

4. s______ (spalten)

55

1. cut, cut, cut
2. burst, burst, burst
3. put on, put on, put on
4. split, split, split

Bei folgenden Verben findest Du solche, deren 2 Vergangenheitsformen gleich sind, und andere, deren Past Participle mit einem -n endet. S c h r e i b e die Verben in die richtige Spalte mit ihren 3 Formen!

~~feed~~ – ~~show~~ – bend – flee – draw – sell – sleep – hang – tear – buy – build

56

Verben mit zwei gleichen Vergangenheitsformen	Das Past Participle endet mit einem -n
feed, fed, fed	show, showed, shown
________________	________________
________________	________________
________________	
________________	
________________	
________________	
________________	

bend, **bent, bent** flee, **fled, fled** sell,**sold, sold** sleep, **slept, slept** build, **built, built** hang, **hung, hung** buy, **bought, bought**	draw, drew, drawn tear, tore, torn

57

Welches Verb dieses Kapitels paßt in allen Formen zu folgenden,bereits bekannten Wörtern?

sing	sang	sung
drink	drank	drunk
sp________	sp________	sp________

spring	sprang	sprung

S c h a u Dir zuerst diese Bildergeschichte g e n a u a n !
V e r v o l l s t ä n d i g e dann den L ü c k e n t e x t darunter!

58

When Robin walked along a road he met a butcher. He was sitting on his cart which was __________ (1) by a horse. The butcher __________________ (2) and asked, "Would you like to join me?" Robin ____________ (3) the horse, the cart and the meat. In Nottingham, after Robin had______ (4) the horse it _______________ (5) and __________ (6). Robin ______ (7) the meat in pieces and __________ (8) a pile. He ______________ (9) the sausages and ________ (10) them. The other butchers nearly __________ (11) with anger. One of them ______________ (12) Robin and ________ (13) his clothes. Robin ____________ (14) onto his cart and __________ (15) away. He ________ (16) once more back into the greenwood.

1. drawn 2. bent down 3. bought 4. fed 5. lay down
6. slept 7. cut 8. built (made) 9. hung up 10. sold
11. burst 12. shook 13. tore 14. sprang 15. drove
16. fled

Übersicht

S e t z e die fehlenden Formen e i n !

1. ________ fled ________
2. ________ ________ torn
3. shake ________ ________
59 4. ________ built ________
5. ________ ________ cut
6. ________ ________ bought
7. ________ drew ________
8. spring ________ ________
9. ________ burst ________
10. ________ ________ sold
11. steal ________ ________
12. ________ ________ fed
13. ________ hung ________
14. ________ ________ broken
15. ________ ________ slept
16. bend ________ ________
17. ________ drove ________

1. flee, fled, fled 2. tear, tore, torn 3. shake, shook, shaken 4. build, built, built 5. cut, cut, cut 6. buy, bought, bought 7. draw, drew, drawn 8. spring, sprang, sprung 9. burst, burst, burst 10. sell, sold, sold 11. steal, stole, stolen 12. feed, fed, fed 13. hang, hung, hung 14. break, broke, broken 15. sleep, slept, slept 16. bend, bent, bent 17. drive, drove, driven

Was haben sie soeben getan? S e t z e die fehlenden Wörter e i n ! (Present Perfect)

Benütze diese Wörter: | drive – draw – build – feed |

1. Roy has drawn a nice picture.

2. Nick ______ ___________ the cattle.

60

3. The man with the cowboy-hat ______ ___________ the car.

4. Jill: "Who ______ ___________ this nice sandcastle? "

---

2. has fed 3. has driven 4. has built

S c h a u Dir zunächst folgende 4 B i l d e r a n ! In den Sätzen daneben erfährst Du Genaueres darüber. Es sind Sätze in der Leideform (im Passiv). Benütze das Past Participle, also die 3. Form!

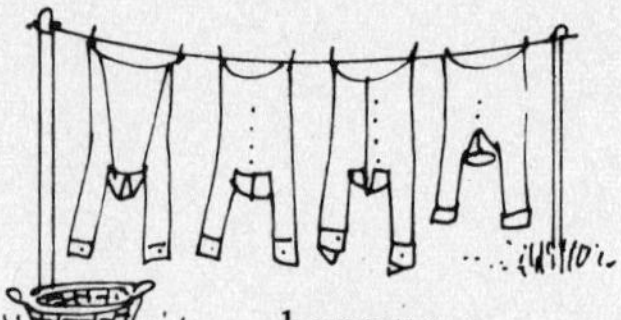

hang up

1. These shirts were hung up
in the morning.

break

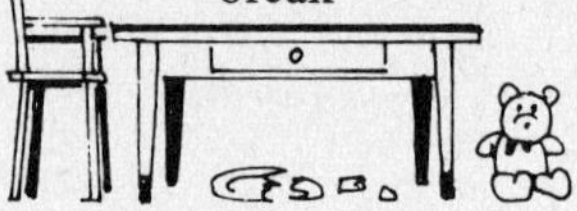

2. This plate was ____________ by Nelly.

61

shake

3. This plum-tree was ____________ by
Dick and Lilly.

steal

4. These cassette recorders were ____________
by Bob Ellison.

V e r v o l l s t ä n d i g e folgenden M e r k s a t z :

In Passivsätzen benützt man immer das ______________________ .

2. broken 3. shaken 4. stolen
. . . benützt man immer das **Past Participle**.

Zwischentest E

S e t z e die fehlenden Verben in den Antwortsätzen e i n !

1 Did an ox or a horse draw the butcher's cart?

A horse ________ the cart.

2 What did Robin buy from the butcher?

He ____________ the cart, his clothes, simply everything.

3 To whom did Robin sell the sausages and meat?

He _________ them mainly to poor people.

4 When did Robin feed his horse?

He _______ it when he had arrived at the market.

5 Did the people or the other butchers break his table?

The other butchers __________ it.

What a surprise for the Tuckers when they came back from holiday this year.
(S e t z e in folgenden Passivsätzen das Past Participle e i n !)

steal – break – tear – cut – bend – throw

6. The window-bars were ________ .

7. The window was ___________ .

8. Three armchairs were ______ .

9. The curtains were __________ .

Fortsetzung nächste Seite!

10. All the records and a lot of books were __________ on the floor.

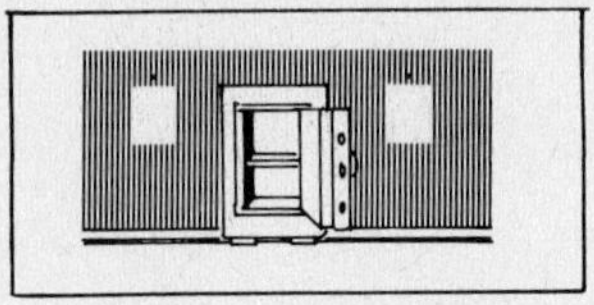

11. All the pictures and the money were __________

There were robbers in their house, I'm afraid.

Was **geschah soeben**? W ä h l e aus dem Rahmen die richtigen Verben und s e t z e das **Present Perfect** e i n !

drive – build – flee – shake – sleep – hang – spring

12. Dagmar ________ __________ the apples on the Christmas tree.

13. Judy ________ __________ in the hammock.

14. The squirrel ________ ________ from the dog.

15. It ________ __________ onto the lowest branch of the tree.

16. Kevin ________ __________ the bottle before he opened it.

17. Steve ________ __________ the van.

18. Johnny ________ __________ this crane by himself.

Die **Lösungen** findest Du am **Ende** dieses Programms.

6. HOW ROBIN WON A NEW FRIEND

One day when the sun was shining hot in Sherwood Forest, Robin came to a little river. On the opposite side of the river he saw a man who was sitting on the trunk of a tree and who was eating a hot venison joint that was still smoking from the fire. He was wearing a long brown habit which showed that he was a friar. Robin placed an arrow to his bow-string and shouted, "Hey, you there, friar! Come and carry me across the river." The large man laid his meat aside, waded through the water, and took Robin on his back.

gegenüberliegende
Baumstumpf
Wildbretkeule
Kutte
Mönch
Bogensehne
watete

When they came to the middle of the river the friar suddenly gave a heave and Robin fell into the water. Coming to the surface, Robin found that the friar had already returned to the trunk and had sat down with his meat once more in his hands. Robin swam back to the bank from where he had started and blew on his horn. He then fired one arrow after another which flew toward the friar who happily caught each one with his buckler and was unhurt.

Ruck
Oberfläche
Ufer
Schild / unverletzt

When Robin stopped shooting the friar found enough time to whistle with his fingers and in response a pack of dogs rushed forward. Robin's friends, who had arrived in the meantime, shot their arrows at the dogs who cleverly managed to avoid being struck and who then carried the arrows back to the friar. One of the dogs swam across the river and nearly bit Robin on the leg. But fortunately, just

pfeifen / Hundemeute
inzwischen
wichen aus

at this moment, Will the Bowman arrived and shouted, "Call off your dogs, Friar Tuck!"	rufe zurück
"Friar Tuck?" cried Robin in astonishment.	überrascht
"Are you Friar Tuck? I was on my way to ask you to join our band."	sich anschließen
"So you're Robin Hood," said the friar. "Well, if I had known, I would have carried you across the river as often as you wished." The two then shook hands, sat on the log, ate a nice meal together, and admired the sun as it shone on the leaves across the river.	Holzbalken / bewunderten / Blätter

---

Suche aus dem Text die fehlenden Formen und setze sie ein!
Lies, wenn nötig, im Text nochmal nach!

1

catch	____________	caught
fangen	fing	gefangen

The friar ____________ each arrow with his buckler.

2

lay	____________	laid
legen	legte	gelegt

The tall man ____________ his meat aside.

3

hurt	hurt	____________
verletzen	verletzte	verletzt

The friar was not ____________ .

---

1. caught 2. laid 3. hurt

4

shine	___________	shone
scheinen	schien	geschienen

The sun ___________ on the leaves of the trees.

5

bite	___________	bitten
beißen	biß	gebissen

The friar's dogs nearly ___________ Robin on his leg.

63

6

eat	___________	eaten
essen	aß	gegessen

Robin Hood and Friar Tuck ___________ a nice meal together.

7

swim	___________	swum
schwimmen	schwamm	geschwommen

Robin ___________ back to the bank where he had come from.

4. shone 5. bit 6. ate 7. swam

In jedem Rahmen sind Verben, die etwas gemeinsam haben.
E r g ä n z e die Lücken und s c h r e i b e ihre Gemeinsamkeit darunter!

	Simple Past	Past Participle
1. sit	___________	___________
2. catch	___________	___________
3. find	___________	___________
4. lay	___________	___________
5. shine	___________	___________

Gemeinsamkeit:

____

____

____

	Simple Past	Past Participle
6. take	took	___________
7. bite	bit	___________
8. fall	fell	___________
9. shake	shook	___________
10. eat	ate	___________

Gemeinsamkeit:

____

____

____

64

1. sat, sat
2. caught, caught
3. found, found
4. laid, laid
5. shone, shone

Gemeinsamkeit:

Simple Past und Past Participle sind **gleich** .

(Auch sinngemäße Antworten sind richtig.)

6. taken
7. bitten
8. fallen
9. shaken
10. eaten

Gemeinsamkeit:

Das Past Participle endet mit **-en.**

65

S u c h e auch hier die Gemeinsamkeiten!

	Simple Past	Past Participle
1. drink	________	________
2. begin	________	________
3. sing	________	________
4. swim	________	________

Gemeinsamkeit:

____

____

____

	Simple Past	Past Participle
5. split	________	________
6. cut	________	________
7. put	________	________
8. hurt	________	________

Gemeinsamkeit:

____

____

1. drank, drunk
2. began, begun
3. sang, sung
4. swam, swum

Simple Past mit **-a-**; Past Participle mit **-u-**.

5. split, split
6. cut, cut
7. put, put
8. hurt, hurt

Alle **drei Formen** sind **gleich**.

66

S e t z e die Verben im Simple Past e i n !

Robin shouted, "Hey, friar! Come and carry me across the river." Friar Tuck ________ (legte) (1) his meat aside, ________ (kam) (2) through the water and ________ (nahm) (3) Robin on his back. In the middle of the river, however, he gave a heave and Robin ________ (fiel) (4) into the water. Robin ________ (schwamm) (5) back to his bank and ________ (blies) (6) his horn. Then he ________ (schoß) (7) one arrow after the other towards the friar. But he ________ (fing) (8) each one with his buckler. One dog ________ (schwamm) (9) across the river and nearly ________ (biß) (10) Robin on his leg. Just at this moment Will the Bowman arrived and shouted, "Call off your dogs, Friar Tuck." Robin and Friar Tuck ________ (schütteln sich) (11) hands and ________ (aßen) (12) a nice meal together. The sun ________ (schien) (13) warm on the leaves and on the water.

1. laid (put)	2. came	3. took	4. fell
5. swam	6. blew	7. shot	8. caught
9. swam	10. bit	11. shook	12. ate
13. shone			

Übersicht

S e t z e die fehlenden Formen e i n !

1. fangen:	catch	________	________
2. legen:	________	laid	________
3. scheinen:	________	________	shone
4. verletzen:	________	hurt	________
67 5. essen:	________	________	eaten
6. schwimmen:	swim	________	________
7. beißen:	________	bit	________

- V e r g l e i c h e zuerst s o r g f ä l t i g mit den Lösungen!
- Decke dann die zwei Vergangenheitsformen ab und s p r i c h l e i s e die drei Formen!
- Arbeite erst weiter, wenn Du sie a u s w e n d i g sagen kannst!

---

1. catch, caught, caught
2. lay, laid, laid
3. shine, shone, shone
4. hurt, hurt, hurt
5. eat, ate, eaten
6. swim, swam, swum
7. bite, bit, bitten

S e t z e bei folgenden Passiv-Sätzen die fehlenden Verben e i n !

Frage: Welche Verbform mußt Du benützen? Simple Past oder Past Participle?

Antwort: ______________________________

This lion was ___________ by a famous zoo director.
⟨fangen⟩

68

This woman was ___________ by a very dangerous snake.
⟨beißen⟩

This tamer was ___________ by one of his lions.
⟨verletzen⟩

Antwort: Past Participle (In Passiv-Sätzen wird immer das Past Participle benützt.)

1. caught 2. bitten 3. hurt

69

What **have** they **just done?**

1. These two polar bears ________ ________ three buckets of fish.

2. This elk ________ ________ across the river.

3. The zoo keeper ________ ________ the mice in the owl's cage.

Kreuze die richtige Antwort an! Die Sätze dieses Lernschritts stehen im

☐ Simple Past
☐ Passiv
☐ Present Perfect

---

1. have eaten 2. has swum 3. has laid

Die Sätze stehen im

☐
☐
☒ **Present Perfect**

Du erkennst das Present Perfect am

have
has + **Past Participle**

Zwischentest F

F i l l in the missing verbs.

1 What did Friar Tuck do when Robin Hood saw him first?

He ______ a hot venison joint.

2 What did the friar do before he waded through the river?

He ________ his meat aside.

3 Did the sun shine or did it rain on the day when Robin met Friar Tuck?

The sun __________ .

4 How did Friar Tuck catch the arrows?

He ____________ them with his buckler.

L o o k at the pictures first. Then f i l l i n the verbs in the proper form.

5. This footballer was ________ by the centre forward.

6. Mr Jackson ______ ________ across the lake.

7. This dog __________ our neighbours' little son last week.

Die **Lösungen** findest Du am **Ende** dieses Programms.

Alphabetische Übersicht der in diesem Programm behandelten unregelmäßigen Verben

Grundform	Simple Past	Past Participle	deutsch
beat	beat	beaten	schlagen, besiegen
become	became	become	werden
begin	began	begun	beginnen
bend	bent	bent	(sich) beugen
bite	bit	bitten	beißen
blow	blew	blown	blasen
break	broke	broken	brechen
build	built	built	bauen
burst	burst	burst	bersten, explodieren
buy	bought	bought	kaufen
can	could	- - - - - -	können
catch	caught	caught	fangen
come	came	come	kommen
creep	crept	crept	kriechen
cut	cut	cut	schneiden
draw	drew	drawn	ziehen, zeichnen
drink	drank	drunk	trinken
drive	drove	driven	fahren, treiben
eat	ate	eaten	essen
fall	fell	fallen	fallen
feed	fed	fed	füttern
fight	fought	fought	kämpfen
find	found	found	finden
flee	fled	fled	fliehen
fly	flew	flown	fliegen
forget	forgot	forgotten	vergessen
get	got	got	bekommen
give	gave	given	geben
go	went	gone	gehen
grow	grew	grown	wachsen, anbauen
hang	hung	hung	hängen
hear	heard	heard	hören
hide	hid	hidden	verstecken
hold	held	held	halten
hurt	hurt	hurt	verletzen
keep	kept	kept	(be-)halten
know	knew	known	wissen, kennen

Grundform	Simple Past	Past Participle	deutsch
lay	laid	laid	legen
leave	left	left	verlassen
lie	lay	lain	liegen
lose	lost	lost	verlieren
make	made	made	machen
meet	met	met	treffen
put	put	put	legen, stellen
run	ran	run	laufen, rennen
say	said	said	sagen
see	saw	seen	sehen
sell	sold	sold	verkaufen
shake	shook	shaken	schütteln
shine	shone	shone	scheinen
shoot	shot	shot	schießen
show	showed	shown	zeigen
sing	sang	sung	singen
sink	sank	sunk	sinken
sit	sat	sat	sitzen
sleep	slept	slept	schlafen
spend	spent	spent	verbringen, ausgeben
split	split	split	spalten
spring	sprang	sprung	springen
steal	stole	stolen	stehlen
strike	struck	struck	schlagen
swear	swore	sworn	schwören, fluchen
swell	swelled	swollen	(an-)schwellen
swim	swam	swum	schwimmen
swing	swung	swung	schwingen
take	took	taken	nehmen, (hin-)bringen
teach	taught	taught	lehren
tear	tore	torn	zerreißen, zerren
tell	told	told	erzählen, sagen
throw	threw	thrown	werfen
wear	wore	worn	(Kleidung) tragen
win	won	won	gewinnen

In diesem Programm verwendete **Fachausdrücke**

deutsch	**lateinisch**	**englisch**	**Beispiel**
Zeitwort	Verb	Verb	see
Grundform	Infinitiv	Infinitive	(to) see
Vergangenheit	Präteritum	Simple Past	saw
Vollendete Gegenwart	Perfekt	Present Perfect	**I have seen** . . .
Mittelwort der Vergangenheit	Partizip Perfekt	Past Participle	seen
Leideform	Passiv	Passive Voice	**He was seen** . . .

Lösungen zu den **Zwischentests**

Zwischentest A (nach Lernschritt 9)

1. spent 2. showed 3. taught (told) 4. told 5. wore 6. came 7. said 8. went

9. made 10. kept 11. threw 12. grew

0–1 Fehler: sehr gut
2–3 Fehler: gut
4 und mehr Fehler: Lernschritt 1–9 nochmal durcharbeiten!

Zwischentest B (nach Lernschritt 21)

1. met 2. took 3. shot (killed with) 4. hid 5. crept

6. has swung 7. has found 8. has fallen 9. have lost

10. could 11. ran 12. gave 13. knew

0–1 Fehler: sehr gut
2–3 Fehler: gut
4 und mehr Fehler: Lernschritt 10–21 nochmal durcharbeiten!

Zwischentest C (nach Lernschritt 39)

1. got 2. saw 3. struck 4. won 5. swore

6. has sung 7. has split 8. have left 9. have drunk 10. has flown

11. beat 12. began 13. put on 14. sat

0–1 Fehler: sehr gut
2–3 Fehler: gut
4 und mehr Fehler: Lernschritt 22–39 nochmal durcharbeiten!

Zwischentest D (nach Lernschritt 48)

1. fought (beat) 2. fell 3. blew 4. heard

5. swollen 6. lay 7. sank 8. took

0 Fehler: sehr gut
1–2 Fehler: gut
3 und mehr Fehler: Lernschritt 40–48 nochmal durcharbeiten!

Zwischentest E (nach Lernschritt 61)

1. drew 2. bought 3. sold 4. fed 5. broke

6. bent 7. broken 8. cut (torn) 9. torn 10. thrown 11. stolen

12. has hung 13. has slept 14. has fled 15. has sprung 16. has shaken
17. has driven 18. has built

0–1 Fehler: sehr gut
2–3 Fehler: gut
4 Fehler: noch gut
5 und mehr Fehler: Lernschritt 49–61 nochmal durcharbeiten!

Zwischentest F (nach Lernschritt 69)

1. ate 2. laid (put) 3. shone 4. caught | 5. hurt 6. has swum 7. bit

0 Fehler: sehr gut
1–2 Fehler: gut
ab 3 Fehler: Lernschritt 62–69 nochmal durcharbeiten!

Lösungen zum **Abschlußtest**

1. went 2. fed 3. took 4. left 5. spent

6. seen 7. broken 8. lost 9. met 10. got 11. sunk 12. said

13. won	14. won	15. gewinnen
16. sleep	17. slept	18. schlafen
19. tell	20. told	21. sagen, erzählen
22. become	23. become	24. werden

0–1 Fehler: Du hast hervorragend gearbeitet!
2 Fehler: Du hast sehr gut gearbeitet!
3 Fehler: Du hast gut gearbeitet!
4 Fehler: Recht ordentlich!
5 Fehler: Hast Du auch immer sorgfältig gearbeitet?

6 Fehler: Ich hoffe nicht, daß Du so viele Fehler gemacht hast! Wenn ja, dann solltest Du nochmal das ganze Programm gewissenhaft durcharbeiten!